Play It Again, Moriarty!

Play It Again, Moriarty!

DEBRETT'S FURTHER GUIDE TO UNRULY BEHAVIOUR

ANDREW MELSOM

Illustrations by Charlotte Christian

DEBRETT'S PEERAGE LTD

Published by Debrett's Peerage Limited,
73-77 Britannia Road, London S.W.6.

First published 1982

ISBN 0 905649 57 5

Designed by Addy Pritchard

Typeset by Capital Letters (W.1)

Printed and Bound in Great Britain by
The Garden City Press Limited
Letchworth, Hertfordshire SG6 1JS

For Sam
a very special black labrador

Contents

WORD GAMES

ROUND AND TEAM GAMES

GAMES WITH A SURPRISE

MAD DOGS AND ENGLISHMEN

FOOLHARDY GAMES

Introduction

Much was said about the publication of *Are You There Moriarty?* last year, most of it complimentary. But there was a fixation about the last chapter in the book, entitled 'Smutty Games', and in particular about a game called 'Bottoms' (page 105). This required the gentlemen to be blindfolded and to pick out their spouses in an identity parade of posteriors. Sir John Junor, in the *Sunday Express,* said 'I welcome a book which gives peasants like myself an authentic insight into the sort of party game played in stately homes. Wouldn't it be marvellous to see the puzzled look on the face of a blindfolded player who advances on a kilted member of the Auchtermuchty Curling Club?'

Bottoms, at its best, is not at all smutty. Linda Lee Potter was altogether nearer the mark when she said, 'I'm amazed that anyone can be so daft'. People enjoy being daft. Letting the hair down is half the fun of after-dinner and house party entertainment. The editor of *The Tatler,* in reference to party games in general, was quoted as saying, 'You need a very low-level sense of humour'. I can only agree with her. But, just to avoid Tina Brown saying the same about this book, you will find that the first chapter is on Word Games, should your guests be of an intellectually active nature. A game of Botticelli could keep the cogwheels turning all night long. I liked what Jenny Rees had to say in the *Daily Express:* 'Games help you keep warm, stave off boredom and create a jolly ambiance'. Perhaps Simon Carr hit the nail on the head in *Monocle:* 'Hair is let down by the tressful. Shy girls will blossom, quiet young men will shine, the old will be invigorated and the young inspired. No matter how difficult the social intercourse, these games are the social lubricant.'

Here are many more ways to oil the wheels of your party. As well as the Word Games you will find a selection of Round and Team games for when things become a little more lively. There are some Games with a Surprise to take over from the Horrid Games in *Are You There Moriarty?.* If your dog enjoys playing games, you will find seven ways in which he can fulfil his role in the house party in Mad Dogs and Englishmen. As well as some ordinarily Foolhardy Games, there are some Frivolous Games for the more rowdy occasion. Finally, at the end of the book, is a chapter titled Most Wicked Deeds. The house-party jape is alive and well and should encourage some really appalling behaviour. If you ever wanted to know what young officers get up to in the Mess, there are also some authentic Mess Games which you can play at home.

I would like to thank everyone who has helped me to compile this book, particularly Andrew Graham, and Charlotte Christian, who, as well as collecting games, has provided another hilarious selection of illustrations to embellish *Play It Again Moriarty!*

ANDREW MELSOM 1982

Word Games

Word Games

All the games in this chapter are ideal as 'icebreakers' and can be enjoyed by people of all ages.

Botticelli

The players sit round a room and make themselves comfortable, for Botticelli is a game which can go on for a very long time. Someone begins the game by assuming the identity of a character from history, male or female, or a character from a book. The game starts by the person introducing himself. We will assume that he has decided to be Tarzan. He then announces to the rest of the players, "I am 'T'". Going round the room the rest of the players then ask 'Botticelli' indirect questions to try and discover his identity. Thinking of 'T', the first player's indirect question may be, "Are you well-versed in the English language?" Botticelli then racks his brains for a poet whose name begins with 'T'. If he succeeds, his reply may be, "No, I am not Tennyson", in which case it is the next player's turn to ask an indirect question. If 'Botticelli' cannot think of a poet whose name begins with 'T', then the player who asked the question earns the right to ask a direct question, to which 'Botticelli' is obliged to answer either 'Yes' or 'No'. A good tip for the first direct question is to ask, "Are you fact?" In our case the answer would be 'No.' A good second direct question to ask is "Are you a man?" In this case the answer has to be 'Yes'. Now players have established that the 'Botticelli' is both male and fictional. In the unlikely event of one of the players suspecting that Tarzan is the identity of 'Botticelli', he may ask, "Are you an inhabitant of the jungle who swings from tree to tree with Cheetah in hot pursuit?" 'Botticelli' will find himself at something of a loss to think of anyone other than Tarzan who had this peculiar habit, so his reply would have to be, "Yes, I am Tarzan". Players will quickly develop the knack of posing the most ingenious questions in order to corner the 'Botticelli' and tax his mind. Here are some 'Botticellis' which are almost impossible to guess!

1. St. Paul, because people always forget that he was a Roman, and players will invariably think of Generals and Emperors.

2. Fay Wray, primarily because her name begins with a 'W' and, although a famous film star, not everyone remembers that it was she who formed a special relationship with King Kong in the original film.

3. Mona Lisa, because she existed, and was not just a painting.

Here is a very brief and heavily 'fixed' round to give you the idea.

BOTTICELLI: I am B.
PLAYER 1:   Are you a breaker of records?
BOTTICELLI: No. I am not Roger Bannister.*
PLAYER 2:   Have you a bent for bridges?
BOTTICELLI: (Forgetting Brunel's name) Um, ooh. . .
PLAYER 2:   Are you fact?
BOTTICELLI: Yes.
PLAYER 2:   Are you one for losing your head?
BOTTICELLI: No, I'm not Anne Boleyn.

4

PLAYER 3:	Do you wave your baton in time to the music?
BOTTICELLI:	(Forgetting Leonard Bernstein) Um, ooh. . .
PLAYER 3:	Are you a woman?
BOTTICELLI:	No.
PLAYER 4:	Are you stumped from time to time?
BOTTICELLI:	No, I am not Boycott.
PLAYER 5:	Do you enjoy a drive to cover?
BOTTICELLI:	No, I am not Barlow.
PLAYER 6:	Are you a sturdy member of a Somerset team, inclined to hit the ball rather hard.
BOTTICELLI:	Yes, I'm Botham.

*Botham has broken many records, but if the 'Botticelli' can think of anyone else whose name begins with 'B', then he may continue to mislead the other players as he did on this occasion when he said he wasn't Roger Bannister. You will soon see how this game alone can keep you going all evening. It's perfect for long car journeys too.

Cross Lists

This game has an infinite number of variations, all of which can be devised by you. It is practical to have organised your list before your party begins as this will save time during the evening.

Write a word down a left-hand column and, along the top, write down a number of articles. It can be any word, and the articles can be any articles. Here is an example.

5

	Actor	Plant	Country	Christian Name	King
B	Bogart	Begonia	Belgium	Bernard	Basil
R		Rose	Russia	Roger	Richard
E			England	Edward	Ethelred
A				Alexander	Arthur
T					Theodore
H					

The list should be divided into boxes and each guest should be given a copy. On the word 'go', everyone tries to fill in as many boxes as he can. The winner is the person who completes the list first. I have filled in some of the boxes above to give you the idea.

Alphabetting

Here is another list game which is a little harder than Cross Lists. Give everyone a piece of paper and a pencil and ask them all to write the alphabet downwards on the left hand side of the page. Then make up a sentence, any sentence, and ask them to write it downwards next to the alphabet. A sentence with roughly twenty-six letters will be a help, but it's not absolutely necessary. On the word 'go', ask everyone to fill in the names of as many people as they can on their list with the initials which have been created. The people can either be famous, or known to all the people playing the game. Here is an example.

A	T	Alfred Tennyson
B	H	Barry Humphries
C	E	Clint Eastwood
D	B	Dirk Bogarde
E	O	
F	Y	
G	S	George Sanders
H	T	
I	O	Ian Ogilvy
J	O	Joe Orton
K	D	Ken Dodd
L	O	Laurence Olivier
M	N	Motilal Nehru
N	T	Norman Tebbitt
O	H	Oliver Hardy
P	E	
Q	B	Quentin Blake
R	U	Richard Usborne
S	R	Samuel Rogers
T	N	
U	I	
V	N	Vita Nicolson
W	G	William Grace
X	D	
Y	E	
Z	C	

I have filled in some names to give you the idea. This is how the game is scored: one point for a name which no one else has on his list, two points for an exceptionally good name. For instance, in the above list, if anyone could put the initials X and D together to make a famous name, then that would certainly score two points. Minus five points for each name which appears on any other list. This means that everyone who has included this name will lose five points. It's perfectly possible at the end of a round for most of the players to have minus points. After a few rounds, players will learn not to put down a name which they believe will crop up on several other lists. Alphabetting gives rise to much 'post mortem' discussion after every game. The winner is the person with the highest score.

Word Bombing

In this game someone begins by saying a letter out loud. The next player must then add another letter to it without completing a word. It can become particularly sadistic, as, once a word looks as if it is being constructed, players can

DELIGHTED

trap another player, or 'bomb' him into completing the word. On the other hand, it may be possible for the player one on in the line from the player being 'bombed' ingeniously to lengthen the word, should his vocabulary be good enough. The buck is then passed on to someone else. Here's a quick round.

PLAYER 1: D
PLAYER 2: E
PLAYER 3: L
PLAYER 4: I
PLAYER 5: G
PLAYER 6: H
PLAYER 1: T
PLAYER 2: E
PLAYER 3: D

So, Player 3 loses. Player 1 would have lost had it not been for Player 2's ability to lengthen the word, thus forcing Player 3 to lose. It should be agreed at the outset of the game that the letters 'I' and 'A' should not be used to start a game.

Initials

Before your party, write down the initials of four films, four songs and four books. Form teams and set a time limit for each team to write down as many of the full titles as they can guess. Here is a suggested list.
FILMS
1. A D A T R   A Day At The Races
2. A Y E W T K A All You Ever Wanted To Know
   S B W A T A   About Sex But Were Afraid To
                  Ask

| 3. T O S O M | The Other Side Of Midnight |
| 4. O F O T C N | One Flew Over The Cuckoo's Nest |

SONGS
1. W C	White Christmas
2. S F	Strawberry Fields
3. F I L A	Falling In Love Again
4. B O T W	Bridge Over Troubled Water

BOOKS
1. O D O Q	Oxford Dictionary Of Quotations
2. B R	Brideshead Revisited
3. F F T M C	Far From The Madding Crowd
4. W T P	Winnie The Pooh

You can, of course, use other categories to suit the company. A party well-versed in classical music may wish to play rounds with the initials of well-known, or not so well-known, operas or ballets.

Syllable Switch

Players sit in a circle and one person begins by saying a word. The next player in the circle must try and think of another word which begins with the last syllable of the previous word. A game could go like this:

PLAYER 1: Necessity
PLAYER 2: Teapot
PLAYER 3: Pottering
PLAYER 4: Ringleader
PLAYER 5: Erasmus

Eliminate players who cannot continue and then begin the game from the next person on in the circle.

Bananas

This is a very silly word game in which players select a word which may have two or three meanings, while another player has to try and guess what the word is. To confuse things further, in their conversation with the player endeavouring to discover the word, players substitute the word 'bananas' for the real word.

One player leaves the room to allow time for the remaining players to choose a word with more than one meaning. For example, the words 'dear/deer'. The conversation may go thus:

HE: Are you going away this year?

PLAYER: Oh, bananas me, I haven't made any plans as yet.

HE: (to the next player) What's your favourite sport?

PLAYER: Well, I must say, I'm very fond of bananas shooting.

HE: (to the next player) What kind of car do you drive?

PLAYER: The car I'd like to drive is too bananas, but at the moment it's a Fiat.

At this stage, unless the guessing player is extremely low on grey matter, he will have discovered the word. This may seem a particularly obvious example, but it is much less obvious to the person guessing.

Here are some other suitable words: great, grate, grate

11

(verb); bear, bear (verb), bare; note (as a verb or noun); break, brake.

Table-jumping Quiz

The object of this game is not to leap over a table, answering questions as you go, but for teams of players to be presented with a different set of problems at a series of tables around the house and, spending about five minutes at each, set out to solve them.

Arrange a number of small tables around the house with three or four chairs around each. On each table place a card with a number of questions on it. The questions on each card should be specific to a particular subject. For example, there could be a literary table, a cinema table, a geography table and a history table.

The questions may look something like this:

TABLE 1
1. Name as many works as you can by E.M. Forster.
2. Name as many Arabian Nights characters as you can.
3. Name as many Spanish authors as you can.
4. Who wrote the following *The Art of the Possible, Burgess and Maclean, Les Miserables, The House on the Strand, Swallows and Amazons.*

TABLE 2
1. Which cowboy was repeatedly asked to come back and didn't?
2. Howard Hawkes told Ernest Hemingway, "I can make a hit film out of your worst novel". He did, what was the name of the book and subsequent film?
3. Name three films which have been remade.
4. Which famous stars have the following initials: G.G.,

12

G.C., C.G., F.A., H.B., M.W., R.R., V.L., M. O'H?

TABLE 3
1. What is the capital of Chile?
2. Write down as many of the United States of America as you can remember.
3. Name a town on the Gulf of Mexico.
4. What is the capital of Iceland? (Extra points if spelled correctly).

TABLE 4
1. Which Wyatt rebelled?
2. Which year was the Indian Mutiny?
3. Why did the Duke of Clarence finish up a bit pickled?
4. When was the armistice signed after World War 1?

Vary your subjects to suit your party and, as far as possible, divide up the talents as equally as possible. Each team should take a pencil and paper around with them to make a list of its answers, and a timekeeper should be elected to ensure that all the teams move on after every five minutes have elapsed. Award one point for every correct answer.

What's in a Name?

Before the game begins, write down the names of all the people in the room. Then create a number of teams of about three or four in each. Announce the first name on the list and, on the word 'Go', the teams should try and construct the most appropriate anagram for the person concerned. An anagram of my name is Drew an Moslem. This is entirely inappropriate, and would score very few marks. Continue until all the names have been completed and award the prize to the team which have consistently displayed the greatest wit.

Moses In The Bulrushes

The object here is to conceal someone, or his name, within a sentence, and your neighbour must try to uncover it. Usually the hiding is more difficult than the finding.

Everyone has a pencil and paper, and time is allowed for them to make up a sentence and to conceal a Christian name within it. When the sentences are complete, the pieces of paper are passed to the right, so that everyone has a name to uncover.

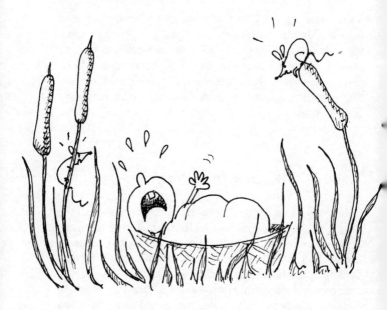

Here are just two examples to give you the idea.

1. I have three main crops in this farm, and I list them in order of profitability; wheat, then rye, then barley.
The sentence conceals Henry.

2. You turn out of Shaftesbury Avenue and into the dreaded Wardour Street traffic.
The sentence conceals Edward.

If the circumstances necessitate the nomination of a winner, you can eliminate any player who fails to compose a sentence or spot a name.

Round and Team Games

Round and Team Games

Here are a variety of games which can be played either in teams or with each player around a room participating in turn.

Zip

This game can be played in a variety of ways. Here are just two of them to give you the idea, with the horrid version first.

A leader begins by reading out the horrifying symptoms of a disease from a medical journal or dictionary. Instead of screaming out the name of the disease when they think they know the answer, players should instead shout the word 'Zip!' There is no radical explanation why this is done, it is just the way the game is played. The temptation to shout out the name of the disease is enormous, and the penalty is disqualification. Here is a round as an example.

LEADER: A disorder of the body's metabolism in which the normal disposal of uric acid is disrupted. This causes pain and inflammation.

PLAYER: Zip!

LEADER: What is the disease?

PLAYER: Gout.

LEADER: Correct.

You can also play a film version of Zip like this:

LEADER: A film directed by Robert Altman about an

American mobile surgical hospital during
the Korean war.

PLAYER: Zip!
LEADER: What is the film?
PLAYER: M.A.S.H.
LEADER: Correct.

The player who succeeds in guessing the correct answer
earns the right to become leader and ask the next question.

Earth, Air and Water

The object of this game is for players to remember, very
quickly, the names of animals which inhabit the above
realms, hence no 'Fire' in the title.

    Players sit in a tight circle and one person begins the
game by throwing a handkerchief at another. As he does

so, he shouts out the name of one of the realms. The person who receives the handkerchief must instantly respond with the name of an animal which lives there. Eliminate players from the ring who fail to respond immediately, use the name of an animal for a second time or suggest that a giant panda can fly.

Subject and Object

The idea of Subject and Object is for two people to leave the room and select a subject and an object. They then return to the room, one representing the subject and the other the object, and the remaining players question them as to their identity. They may only answer 'Yes' or 'No' to the questions asked. Here are some examples of subjects and objects: Roy Rodgers and Trigger, The Queen and Buckingham Palace, Malvolio and his green cross-garters. The subjects and objects should always be connected in some way.

Walter Raleigh Races

Select two teams with equal numbers of ladies and gentlemen. Give each gentleman a sack (a cloak) and set a course for the two teams with a point A and a point B. On the word 'go', the gentleman in the first pair lays down his sack at the lady's feet, she runs along it and steps just off the end. He picks it up and lays it down again in front of her feet. She runs along it once more, he picks it up and puts it down again until they reach point B. If the lady deliberately steps beyond the forward edge of the sack or if the gentleman lays it down well in front of her toes they are

21

disqualified. On arrival at point B, the second pair in each team, as in a relay, take up the race going to point A where they are replaced by the third pair, who race to point B. This continues until all the pairs have completed the course.

Blowing The Top

A complete pack of cards is placed on top of a bottle. The object is for all the players to sit around the bottle and take it in turns to try and blow a single card off the top of the pack. Any player who blows more than one card off the pack removes one article of clothing. If the whole pack falls off the bottle at least two articles of clothing must come off. There is, needless to say, a knack to this game, and it's advisable to put in some practice if you like winning.

Spare Chair

This is a kind of musical chairs without the music. All the players sit in a circle, leaving one empty chair. 'He' stands in the middle. Everyone seated in the circle then begins to move from place to place, while the 'he' attempts to sit in the empty chair. As the players are constantly moving, so is the vacant space.

When the 'he' eventually manages to secure a seat, the player behind him, who should have taken the place gets up and becomes 'he'. The first 'he' then retires and one chair is removed from the circle. It is a good idea for the host or hostess to be 'he' first, for not only does this appear

to be a sporting gesture but they can then attend to the needs of their guests.

The Game – Peking Style

This is a cross between The Game (see p.46 of *Are You There, Moriarty?*) and Chinese Whispers.

Two teams are made up and are given separate rooms in which to confer. Team A decides on an elaborate sequence of events. For instance: a man in a boat sees a girl in another boat. He cannot take his eyes off her. His enthusiasm is dampened because he fails to see a man, equally thrilled by the girl in the boat, approaching him in a third boat. They collide and both boats capsize. A shark gobbles them both up.

The first member of Team B is then called into the room and told the sequence, once only, as in Chinese Whispers. It is then his job to call in the second member of Team B and act out the entire sequence to his colleague. Unlike The Game, the second member of Team B may ask nothing to help him ascertain the content of the sequence. When the first member of Team B has finished acting, the second member must call in the third, and act out what he interpreted from the performance given to him. The sequence continues until the last member of Team B has seen a performance, who then tells everyone present what he deduced from it. The results of this game are always hilarious and never bear any similarity with the original story.

If the occasion necessitates a winner, then it is the team whose story most resembles the original sequence after all its members have performed.

Wink Pick-up

As many couples as there are in the party can play Wink Pick-up, though one lady must remain out of the game at any one time.

Chairs are arranged in a circle and the ladies sit in them. The men stand, one behind each chair, so that one man alone has an empty chair in front of him. He must endeavour to catch the attention of one of the other ladies and 'slip her a wink', whereupon she must immediately leap to her feet and run to sit in the vacant chair. The man guarding her will, if he's quick enough, try and stop her by holding her shoulders, thus pinning her to her seat. There should be no wandering hands in readiness to seize a lady. All arms to the side until there's an attempt by a lady to escape.

Once a lady has escaped, the new gentleman with a vacant chair before him must try and get a lady to fill it by winking around.

When the game is established and everyone is familiar with it, you may wish to swap the ladies and gentlemen around, so the ladies do the winking.

Missing Links

A leader takes his place at the centre of a circle of players. He tells them that he will think for a moment until he has fixed his mind on a certain object. Everyone else is then asked to concentrate hard and see if they can guess what it is that the leader has in mind. They each guess out loud and, when they have all spoken, the leader announces the object about which he was thinking. At this point the leader invites everyone to form some kind of a link, however nebulous, between his object and theirs.

For example, if the leader's object was a 'case', and three of the objects guessed by the other players were; 'globe', 'shoe' and 'picture', these may be the reasonings of the players to link the objects:–

1. A case is essential for travelling the globe.
2. A shoe packs neatly into a case.
3. Anyone with a picture like that is a case for treatment.

Award a prize for the most imaginative link.

Marking Time

If you have a loud ticking clock, it can be amusing to blindfold people, one at a time, and see if they can find the clock and touch it by starting at the other end of the room. Everyone else will have to remain absolutely silent while the game is in progress. Continue until everyone has had a go, moving the clock between each person's turn.

Just Passing Through

Players sit or stand in a circle and an orange is passed through the clothing of everyone in the circle, either up one trouser-leg and down another or, through both sleeves of a coat or jumper. No short cuts are allowed.

The game can be varied by substituting a ball of string so that, at the game's end, everyone is connected to each other.

Lost Memory

At some stage before the game is played you will need to have obtained the contents of someone's pockets or, in the case of a lady, handbag. When you are ready to begin, seat everyone in a circle and announce that someone has been found suffering from loss of memory and that they can each help to identify him or her. Then empty on to a tray the contents of the pocket or handbag and invite everyone, in turn, to identify the owner of the articles. Wit and spice can be added to the occasion by some amusing judgement of the individual's character from the articles.

Famous Meals

There is no real point to Famous Meals. It is a silly round game which any number of people can play.

Without explaining the object of the game, give everyone in the room a piece of paper and ask them to write down the name of one famous person. Then collect the papers, shuffle them and read out a different name to each person in turn. They must each take the initials of their given personality and make up a suitable meal for them. A typical game might go like this:

LEADER:	Leonardo da Vinci
PLAYER:	Leeks, diced carrots and veal
LEADER:	Horatio Nelson
PLAYER:	Ham and nettle soup
LEADER:	Charlie Chaplin
PLAYER:	Corned-beef and courgettes

If you place a time limit on answers, a winner will emerge after a few rounds.

County Council

This game makes excellent practice for everyone who may have to serve on a committee. It is a test of negotiating power which, if the atmosphere is right, can appear very real. Everyone sits round a table and imagines themselves to be councillors serving on a town planning committee, and each person is awarded an area of responsibility. One person may be 'housing', another may be 'street-lighting', another 'sports facilities', 'roads', 'transport' and so on. In the kitty the Corporation has exactly £1,000,000 available to be spent on town projects. Irritatingly, each project costs £500,000. So some councillors will have to lose out. There can be no half measures, a councillor cannot just begin his project with a token £250,000, he must plump for all the money he needs to complete it.

To preside over the meeting a chairman is elected and, since the councillors cannot agree between themselves where the money should be appropriated, it becomes his grim duty to decide which projects are most necessary to the area.

The object of the meeting is for each councillor to make the best argument for his particular project and be so convincing that it becomes quite unnecessary for the chairman to arbitrate. The chairman has to meet the Lord Mayor at a tree-planting ceremony in half an hour, and agreement has to be reached within that time. (15 minutes or 1 hour if you wish, depending on the number of councillors.)

Everyone is given a few moments to decide on their areas of responsibility, the project which is of such tantamount importance and the arguments in favour of it's fulfilment. When everyone is ready, the chairman invites the first councillor to make his case. In a good game, diplomacy should collapse within a few moments and a heated discussion should be followed by angry exchanges. It is the chairman's responsibility to restore peace to the meeting, remembering that an agreement must be reached. Here are three suggested projects.

TITLE	PROJECT	ARGUMENTS
Leisure	New Adventure Playground	More children in area. No facilities at present. Depressed mother figures rising rapidly.

30

Town Hall Warden	New extension	Chairman needs a new office. More clerks needed to administer the rates. Would improve the value of the building.
Prison Services	Prison Football	Other parties could use pitch. Disturbing Press reports about prison facilities. Good for rehabilitation.

Games With A Surprise

Games With A Surprise

All these games are likely to give your guests a small surprise. The first two items, being telepathic games, are surprising in that they are impressive.

The Telepathic Poker

This is a game in which a player pretends to be gifted in the art of telepathy. He suggests that, if he leaves the room, he will be able to pick out an object which has been chosen and agreed by everyone while he was out. He achieves this successfully by an elaborate code known to both him and an accomplice who remains in the room and is therefore familiar with the chosen article.

The accomplice holds a poker or fire-iron, or anything which someone may easily pick up and play with without arousing suspicion. The code involves both speech and the tapping of the poker to indicate vowels.

Here is an example which will explain the code. Assume that the article chosen was a lamp. The telepathic man will be listening at the door. The accomplice will say something like "Let him come in now". This will tell the telepathic man that the word begins with the letter 'L'. All consonants are indicated by the accomplice beginning a sentence with the letter in question. When the telepathic man comes into the room the accomplice will tap his poker once on the ground. This will indicate that the second letter of the article is 'A'. All vowels are indicated by tapping the poker on the ground:

A: 1 tap
E 2 taps
I: 3 taps
O: 4 taps
U: 5 taps.

The accomplice then starts a sentence with the letter 'M':
"Make sure you concentrate hard". Finally the accomplice
might say, "Please everyone be quiet". The telepathic
man will now know that the object is a lamp. He should
then, just for effect, walk over to the lamp and ceremon-
iously touch it.

The Wizard

This is the most sophisticated form of telepathic game I
have encountered. All that is needed is a pack of cards, a
telephone and a patient accomplice.

You mention casually that you have met a marvellous
character called The Wizard who is gifted with most
impressive magical powers. In fact, he can pick a previously
chosen card from a pack and doesn't even have to be in
the same room. Furthermore, he can perform this trick
over the telephone. You then lay out a pack of cards and
invite one of the party to choose one, and show it to
everyone in the room, making very sure that you see it too.
You then go to the telephone and, in the presence of
everyone, you telephone The Wizard. When the telephone is answered, you say, "Can I speak to The Wizard
please?" A few seconds later you say, "Yes, I'll hang on",
and a few moments after that you say, "I would like to
hand you over to my friend". You then hand the receiver
over to the person who has chosen the card, and all he
hears is The Wizard say the name of the card and the

telephone go dead.

This is how it's done. The Wizard is an accomplice with whom you have a pre-arranged code. You tell him that you will be having a party at a certain time and that you wish to perform the trick. When you telephone him and ask to speak to The Wizard, that is his signal to begin

the agreed sequence. Assume that the chosen card was the Knave of Diamonds. The Wizard will say, slowly and audibly, "Spades . . . Hearts . . . Diamonds . . .". As soon as he says Diamonds, you then say, "Yes, I'll hang on". This is then his signal to begin with the numbers. The

Wizard then says, "Ace ... King ... Queen ... Knave ..". As soon as he says the word 'Knave', you then say, "I'll hand you over to my friend". At which point the person who has chosen the card is told exactly what it is.

You may, of course, wish to adopt your own particular code, or be even more sophisticated by changing it each time you telephone. Either way, it is a quite baffling trick and will keep a party mystified for hours.

Snow Blind

Place a coin in a saucer and bury it beneath a generous sprinkling of flour. Invite a friend to take out the coin with his mouth, first blowing on the saucer to make the coin visible. Stand back and watch destiny take its toll.

Another version for the more wary customer is as follows: Invite someone to blow a candle out blindfold, telling him that, each time he succeeds, you will take the candle a little bit further away. You imply that the object of the game is to see who can blow out the candle from the furthest distance when blindfolded. Having chosen your victim, you hold a lighted candle in front of him and ask him to blow hard. Should your victim miss the candle, quickly blow it out, and invite him to have a peep, making sure there is plenty of applause to encourage his supposed success. Play the game once more to reassure the victim that he is involved in, and succeeding at, this trivial diversion. At the third attempt, just as the victim is about to blow, a colleague holds a saucer of flour about in inch away from the victim's mouth.

On no account mention the name of the game in advance or the victim is likely to smell a rat.

Hannibal's Fantastic Journey

This game is completely clean. However, when the lady, and I'm afraid it has to be a lady, removes her blindfold at the end of the game, she should be absolutely horrified. Ask a lady wearing a dress if she would like to recreate Hannibal's fantastic journey across the Alps. Tell her that it's a wonderful experience and have people who know the game standing by to reassure her that this really will be the event of a lifetime.Blindfold her, take her gently by the hand and tell her that you will lead her through this incredible journey. Have some friends standing by to make blizzard-like noises. Then explain to your victim that she is approaching a large plateau. But wait! The ground is opening up beneath her. A crevasse is forming underneath her feet. She must spread her feet wider and wider, or she will disappear into the very core of the mountain. Tell her that it is just a few more steps to the end of the crevasse and that she should continue to walk with her feet apart until you give the word that it's quite safe.

After she has safely negotiated the white hell of the mountains, but before she removes her blindfold, all the men in the party quietly lie down lengthways along the 'crevasse' which she has just straddled. She is then told that the journey is over and she may remove her blindfold. At some later stage the ladies can reassure the victim of the men's completely gentlemanly conduct throughout.

An Easy Wager

Bet anyone that you can drink a pint of water before they can eat two water biscuits. There is no doubt that you will win. Anyone gullible enough to take you on will have a mouthful of biscuit for a very long time.

Egg Head

Tell your victim that you will give him £10 if he will let you crack two eggs over his head. This should appeal to most people as being a messy but easy way of earning a tenner. Break just one egg over your victim's head and give him nothing. He will beg you to crack another one so that he can earn his money. Unfortunately for him, you decline to do so!

Introductions

There is quite a build-up to this particular surprise, for which you need to select about six accomplices. One of these must act as doorkeeper, whose function it is to admit the victims one by one, and also to ensure there is no peeping. They are asked to leave the room and told that they will be invited to return shortly to be introduced to the Fly family. The five other accomplices remain in the room and line up like a football team about to be introduced to a dignitary, starting with a lady, then a man, and then a lady and so on to the end of the line. The second man, who is the fourth in the line, holds a mug of water. The doorkeeper admits the first victim and you greet him with the words, "Allow me to introduce you to the Fly family. Would you mind bowing to the male members of the family and shaking hands with the ladies?"

You lead the victim to the first lady. "This is Butterfly," you say, and signal to your companion that he should shake hands. You then lead him to the next in line: "And this is Blowfly." This time he bows to Blowfly. "This is Dragonfly," you say as you introduce him to the second lady. Then you prepare for the kill. If all goes well, your victim will not be suspicious as there is still one more person in the line and they would expect that, if anything nasty is about to happen, then it will involve the last in the line. "And this," you proclaim, "is Letterfly!" Your victim bows and receives a faceful of water from Letterfly. The mug is then refilled and the doorkeeper invites the next victim to come in, while the first victim conceals himself and watches the remainder of the party get a soaking.

Shock Horror

If you're going to play this game, the best thing is to invite all the people you dislike most to your party. It is extremely nasty. Sit your party in a long line and ensure that all of them are properly blindfolded. Casually explain that someone in the house has been chopped into tiny pieces and that you are about to pass portions of their slimy anatomy down the line. "This is the heart", you explain as you slop a piece of wet liver into the hand of the first-in-line. The first-in-line hurriedly passes the 'heart' on to the second person and so on. There is no winner or loser to this game. There is, in fact, no point to it at all. It's just rather sick.

Here are some more items which you can substitute for parts of the body:

EYES: Grapes or jelly.
HANDS: Rubber gloves soaked in soap.
BRAIN: A hot, wet ball of string.

Mix 'n' Match

This is a great game for cuddlesome doublesomes to display their feelings towards each other after being deprived of each other's intimate company for the whole of dinner.

Quite simply, the lights are turned off and couples are given the task of finding each other in the dark. Not a word must be spoken. Identities must be established by feel alone. A prod here, a squeeze there, but not so much as a whimper must be emitted. Unless absolutely necessary, the obvious areas of familiarity should be avoided. This game is a great test for a spouse's knowledge of what their opposite number was wearing for the evening. Set a time limit and turn on the lights. See who thought who was who. Try and find out why.

Lay Lady Lay

An unsuspecting lady (or gentleman) is seated in a chair facing someone mean enough to play this trick with a cracking twist. The unsuspecting lady (UL), is told to imitate exactly all the animals that the mean person (MP) does. MP begins by becoming a donkey, so UL becomes a donkey too, both making all the relevant noises. MP works his way through a number of animals until UL has loosened up until finally, he becomes a chicken. He flaps up and down squawking as he goes. All this is copied faithfully by UL. As this charade reaches its peak, someone slips an egg underneath UL, and she gets a surprise.

WARNING:– DO NOT USE A GOOD CHAIR

Jaws

Bet someone he will not put a raw egg into his mouth. £5 should tempt someone enough to fall for it. This is £5 which will eventually have to be handed over to the victim, and he will need to be appeased.

Your victim's jaws, no matter how large, will be unable to close on the egg. Just a small tap under the chin will achieve the necessary. Stand well back from the victim.

Zimbali Airways

You may have heard of, or even experienced, the dreaded 'Levitation Game'. This is when some unfortunate person is blindfolded, lifted about three inches into the air on a plank, and told to jump. Because the victim has placed his hands on someone's head, who then squats down on the floor, and the plank is being wobbled convincingly by two strong men, he is made to believe that he's six foot in the air rather than just three inches. Zimbali Airways is a more enjoyable and more elaborate version of the same trick.

A lady or gentleman is led out of the room and told that he or she will be the sole passenger aboard Zimbali Airways, Flight ZA 10, to Mabula. The victim is properly blindfolded and led into the room. Someone must agree to be the pilot or narrator throughout, and putting on his best Idi Amin accent, should continue as follows:

"Dis am de Zimbali Airways flight from Ungarra to Mabula. De weather gonna be pretty fine up dere, so fassen up de ol' seat belt, and we be gettin' off de ground pretty damn quick. Unfortunately deres standin' room only, but never mind de flight gonna be heck of a good ride.

So, fassen' up de seat belt!"

At this point the victim is lead on to a plank and his hands are placed on the shoulders of an accomplice.

"Okay, de seat belts fassened? Good, good. Now we taxiin' toward de take off an' shortly we be zoomin' up de runway."

The two strong gentlemen manning the plank gently manoeuvre it to give the impression that the aircraft has begun to move. The accomplice moves his shoulders slightly.

"Now we turnin' on to de runway."

The two plankmen slowly turn the plank which indicates that the aircraft is turning and ready to take off.

"An' here we go. 5 mile an hour an' gatherin' speed..."

The two plankmen begin to jiggle.

"Now gettin' up to 50 mile an hour . . ."

The plankmen jiggle more vigorously.

"Now goin' so fast, we gonna have to take off. Up, up an' away we go into de blue skies."

Now the accomplice slowly lowers himself so that the

victim feels he is going upwards, and the two plankmen jiggle the plank as if the aircraft was in flight, but keeping the plank just three or four inches off the ground.

"Very sorry, ladies an' gentlemen, but dere seem to be a bit of de bonfire in de engines. But don't panic. It happenin' all de time."

The accomplice heaves his shoulders from side to side to indicate that the aircraft is losing control and the plank is jiggled up and down.

"I'm sorry to report dat de engines now fallin' off altogether. Now we gonna have to bail outa de ol' crate. Unfassen' seat belts an' jump when ready."

Frantic jiggling from the accomplice and the two plankmen and shouts from everyone to jump will encourage the victim to bail out. He will think he's right up in the air. His knees will quiver and he will jump – all of four inches on to the carpet, much to the amusement of everyone present.

Mad Dogs and Englishmen

Mad Dogs and Englishmen

There are proud men who regard their dog's training as sacred. These few frivolous games are not for the likes of them. They could prove ruinous to a dog's discipline and certainly damage the owner's pride.

Go Fetch

There are some dog chocs called Good Boys which, if you have ever mistakenly popped one into your mouth as I have, do not taste as good as they look. Dogs, on the other

49

hand, find them quite irresistible. Should you fail to obtain any Good Boys, Bonios or some of the other canine delicacies will work just as well.

All the dogs staying in the house are assembled in one room. Valuable ornaments are removed and the dogs are told to sit. The Good Boys are waved in front of them for a while and, once there's a good drool going, they are thrown to every corner of the room, in full view of all the dogs. On the word of command, the mad dash begins as each dog races to devour as many Good Boys as he can. The winning dog is the one which collects the most.

Obstacle Race

Prepare or select a number of obstacles around the garden and race teams comprising both men and dogs around the course. For instance — over the oil tank — under the cavalletti — over the five-bar gate — through the hole in the wall and back over the garden shed. First team home gets a pint of beer and a bone.

Relay

Form two teams comprising men and their dogs, of roughly equal athletic ability. A point A and a point B are agreed as being the course the two teams must run. The owners should run the first leg, A to B, dogs run the second leg, B to A, and so on until the first team, both dogs and their owners, has made base. If the dogs are not sufficiently well trained to sit at a word of command, it will be necessary to have dog-holders on duty.

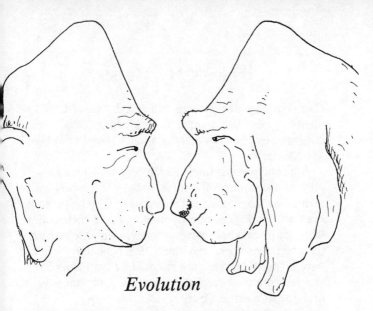

Evolution

The theory is, just as married couples are supposed to grow to look like one another, so are dogs and their owners. In the opinion of a selected panel of judges, which dog most resembles his owner?

Where's My Master?

Can your dog identify your call at a distance? Could he identify your call amid a host of other calls? These questions can be answered by a quick round of Where's My Master?

Some helpers assemble all the dogs which are going to play at the centre of a large field. The owners space themselves about the field's perimeter. The helpers then keep all the dogs secure by holding on to their collars, while the owners have thirty seconds in which to scream at their dog from where they stand. When the thirty seconds have elapsed, the dogs are released by the helpers to go and seek out their respective masters. The winner is the first dog to reach his owner.

How To Read A Dog's Mind

During the course of the evening, preferably after the wine has flowed freely, someone casually mentions that he once met a man who taught him how to read a dog's mind. Some kind of proof will be demanded by the guests, so the 'dog psychologist' must have previously nobbled two accomplices: one to suggest a method of providing unassailable proof, another discreetly to communicate, in an agreed code, the information the 'dog psychologist' will require to amaze his friends.

The first accomplice suggests that a row of eight cards should be laid out on the floor and that the 'dog psychologist' goes out of the room while, in full view of the dog, someone touches one of the cards. When the 'dog psychologist' walks back in to the room, the dog will be able to tell him which card had been touched while he was absent. The second accomplice has, of course, seen which

card was chosen. His agreed code with the 'dog psychologist' should be very simple. If he says, 'Come in, George', this is three words so, the 'dog psychologist' will know it's the third card in the row. If he says, 'Time to come in now, George', this is six words and therefore it will be the sixth card in the row.

The whole charade can be made more credible if the 'dog psychologist' seems to carry on a conversation with his dog when he comes into the room.

A Bit Of Stick

Standing on a bank, owners throw sticks into the water for their dogs. Should a dog fail to return with a stick, the owner must retrieve it himself. The owner of the last dog to return must be thrown a stick to retrieve by one of the other owners.

Foolhardy Games

Foolhardy Games

You are not intended to take any of these games too seriously. At the end of the chapter you will find some equally unserious card games.

Dragons

This game is a wonderful combination of Sardines and Murder in the Dark. The bigger the house, the more difficult the game becomes and the more fun. At least two staircases are needed to allow adequate escape routes

from a roaring Dragon! Someone is elected to be the Dragon. The lights are then turned off, and everyone else runs to hide. After a good few minutes the Dragon sets out to capture and 'freeze' a victim. Once frozen, the victim must stand absolutely still until someone comes to rescue him by touch. Unlike Sardines, the 'frozen' victim can yell for help, as well as warn the rest of the party of the Dragon's whereabouts. The object of the game is for the dragon to 'freeze' everyone and thus render them helpless.

The number of Dragons can be increased according to the number of people playing.

Armchair Table Tennis

Much fun can be had by playing the game to exactly the same rules as conventional Table Tennis, but with both players being obliged to remain seated in a chair or on a stool throughout the game.

Doughnut Races

One of the most difficult things in the world is to eat a doughnut without licking your lips. Involve as many people as there are doughnuts and have a race. Anyone caught licking his lips is disqualified.

A Quick Feel

Blindfold all the players, bring a tray of small familiar objects into the room and let each person in turn spend a short time feeling the objects on the tray. Don't let them mention any of the articles out loud, but let them feel the articles and see how many they can write down on a piece of paper after the tray has been removed. People are often surprised what everyday articles they were unable to recognize by feeling them.

Feel A Farm

You need to have, somewhere in the attic, one of those old toy farms with an abundance of animals which children use to make up their own farmyards. Blindfold players, give them some of the animals and see if they can guess them correctly.

The game can also be played with toy soldiers. Old campaigners can guess, "This is a grenadier", "This is a flame thrower" and so on.

Role Reversal

Anyone who has ever been on one of those tedious seminars where a great deal of time is spent performing an unfamiliar role, so that a greater understanding of such and such a department is achieved, will have the gist of this game.

In this instance, you have races where the ladies are asked to clean a gun or the men are asked to ice a cake. Invent a points system to suit the event, with the men marking the ladies and the ladies marking the men.

Potato Skittles

Parade a number of washing-up liquid bottles at the end of a passage in triangular formation. Give everyone five spuds each and see who can knock over the most bottles with the fewest potatoes.

Apple Bobbing

Fill a dog-bath or washing-up bowl with water and float half a dozen or so apples therein. Two players kneel on either side of the bowl and, on the word 'go', try to lift the apples out of the water with their teeth. The winner is the one who gets the most apples.

News and Weather

You can only play this game if there is a howling gale blowing. It is not unlike 'Not Newspapers' (see page 10 of *Are You There, Moriarty?*). Prepare a number of papers, different editions and different titles, so that they are completely mixed up. Give each team of two or three people, three newspapers which have been jumbled up. Take them out into the garden and get them to put the newspapers back in the right order.

Indoor Football

In this game the goal is a single bottle or upright skittle in the centre of the room. One person is elected goalie and it is his job to stop the bottle from being knocked over. The other players kneel in a circle round the bottle and roll a ball to try and knock the bottle over. Players will develop the art of passing the ball to a player on the opposite side to the ring, thus enabling that player to 'shoot' at the bottle before the goalie has time to spring round in defence. Players should all stay fairly close to one another so that the ball does not go out of the circle and slow up the game. Should the goalie accidentally knock over the bottle, this is reckoned as a goal, and the last player to have had a shot at goal earns the honour of becoming the new goalie. If you want a winner, get someone to check how long each person manages to remain goalie and give a prize to the one who lasted longest after everyone has had a turn in goal.

Dodge

Dodge is not unlike 'Indoor Football', only this time the goalkeeper is the goal as well. He stands in the middle of the room and the remaining players stand as far away as the room will allow. The ball is thrown from person to person, the object being to hit the goalie below the knees. The goalie must try to dodge each shot. As soon as he is hit, he is replaced by the player who made the successful strike. Again, a winner, if needed, can be nominated on a time basis.

Some Foolhardy Card Games

Oh Hell!

Players are seated in a circle and the dealer gives one card from a single deck of cards to each person. The suit of the card at the top of the remaining pack is declared 'trumps'. This card is then inserted somewhere into the pack at random.

Oh Hell! is played in the same fashion as Whist and the object of the game is to get as many tricks as possible. The players must predict at the start of each round how many tricks they are going to win. This is done by banging their fists simultaneously on the table. On the fourth bang the players extend as many fingers as the number of tricks they think they will make.

The scoring works as follows:

+5   For every trick a player forecast he would win.
–5   For every trick the player is out from his forecast.

So if a player forecast he would get 0 and he scores no tricks, then he scores +5 points. If, on the other hand, he wins one trick, he scores –5 points. Each round continues until the pack is finished. The winner deals the next round.

Animal Snap

Before the game begins each player must think up a suitably silly animal noise which will serve to distinguish him or her. Thereafter the game is similar to, but sillier than, snap. All the players are given an equal pile of cards, so, if there are a lot of players, more than one pack can be used. Each player turns a card up simultaneously, one by one. When a player sees a card of the same value as his own, he must complete the following sequence: the chosen animal noise of his opponent twice, his own noise twice, then grab his opponent's pile of cards. His opponent will be trying to do the same, so speed is of the essence.

A player is disqualified when his cards run out, and the winner is the person who ends up with all the cards.

Once the players have established how to play the game, it can be further complicated by stipulating that everyone must have a more elaborate animal noise. Here are some suggestions:

A constipated owl.
A centipede with a stomach ulcer.
A parrot with a pirate on his shoulder.
A warthog in the mating season.

Corks

If there are six people playing Corks, you need to have drunk five bottles of wine before the game, since you need one less cork than there are players. The other requirement is a pack of cards. For six people you need 24 cards:

4 Aces
4 Kings
4 Queens
4 Knaves
4 Tens
4 Nines

The rest of the pack is put away, the 24 cards are then shuffled and dealt. The five corks are placed in the centre of the table. The players pick up their cards and, depending on which card they have most of, they decide which card they are going to collect. When everyone is ready, each player passes one card to the person on his right. The cards continue to pass until a player has 4 of a kind, whereupon he grabs one of the corks. The person who is not able to grab a cork must take off an article of clothing. Continue the game as long as the occasion allows.

Frivolous Games

Frivolous Games

Everything in this Chapter is very silly.

Big Nose

This game is played at a party, particularly a dinner party, where someone is horribly late. It can also be played under the same circumstances at a business meeting. The idea is to victimise the late arrival by making fun of any physical idiosyncrasies he may have. For example, he may have a very large nose. Points are then scored during the course of the evening for introducing the word 'nose' into the conversation in the presence of the late arrival.

Players score one point for saying another word with the same sound like, "No one knows". They score two points for saying the word 'nose' in the correct context and three points for creative insinuations like, "I met a parson". A panel decides at the end of the party who is the overall winner.

Nappy Rush

This is a perfectly simple game. All the men have to do is to dress up in nappies, or be similarly swaddled, and sit cradled in the arms of the ladies. The ladies, if their imagination runs to it, must pretend they are the mothers

PLAM-4

of the monsters submissively curled upon their laps. Each mother is provided with a baby's bottle full of milk, or some suitable alchoholic substitute, and attempts to bottle-feed her charge. The first mother to empty her bottle without any of the contents dribbling down the front of her baby is the winner.

Greedy Chocolate

This game is very frustrating for those who like chocolate, as it involves a most complicated way of eating it. All the players sit down in a circle. In the middle of the circle is a top hat, a large overcoat, a pair of wellies, a bar of chocolate and a knife and fork. One player is elected to begin and is given a dice. Each player is allowed one throw of the dice, the object being to throw a six. As soon as the first player has thrown the dice, he passes it to the left for the next player to throw. When a six is thrown, the lucky player screams, "Chocolate!" and leaps into the middle of the circle. He must then put on all the clothes, grab the knife and fork and try and eat the chocolate square by square. While all this is going on the remaining players are continuing to pass the dice, endeavouring to throw a six. As soon as someone does so, he must leap into the circle and scream, "Chocolate!". At this point the player already in the circle, regardless of his state of dress or progress with the chocolate, must disrobe and the new six-thrower must replace him. The object of Greedy Chocolate, as the title suggests, is to eat as much chocolate as possible before another six is thrown. The winner is the person who finishes the chocolate.

Dingle Dangle

This is a particularly undignified game, so stand by with a camera to capture the precious moments when players take a very unusual, but necessary, stance to complete the game.

Place as many milk bottles as there are players out in a line. Each player should tie one piece of string around his waist and attach a second piece, about 18 inches long, to the first piece. A pencil or biro should be attached to the end of the second piece of string and allowed to hang between the player's legs. All the players stand astride their bottles and endeavour to drop their pencils into their bottles. Award a prize to the person who has given the most amusement to the onlookers.

The Bottle Race

Two teams are chosen and form up in two lines. The leading man in each team is given a bottle which he must grip between his legs. On the word 'go' the first two players waddle forward, climb over a sofa which has been placed across the room, touch the far wall, climb back over the sofa and pass the bottle to the next player. The winning team is the first home, but the game can be made more exciting by awarding time penalties every time a player drops his bottle.

Burst my Balloon

Someone is chosen to be 'he' and is given a balloon filled with water which he must protect from all the other players whose aim is to try and burst it, thus soaking him completely. It should be agreed at the outset that everyone takes a turn at being 'he'.

Pocket Pass

All the men stand behind their chairs along each side of the table. A lady stands behind each man and puts her hands in his trouser pockets. On the word 'go' the two ladies at one end of the line are each given a table mat which they must grip through the material of the man's trousers, transfer the mat to the other hand in the other pocket and then pass it on to the next lady who grips it in the same way and so passes it on. The winning team is the first to get their table mat to the other end of the line. It is not advisable to suggest playing Pocket Pass if you are wearing very tight trousers.

This Is A Rat

These next two games, both of which are played round a table, should reduce your party to fits of uncontrollable laughter. They are both games which require maximum concentration and, played in a restaurant, they will result in dirty looks the like of which you have never seen. Someone picks up an object, passes it to the person on his left and announces that it is some other

This is a Rat!

object. For example, he may pick up a spoon and say to his neighbour, "This is a rat!" The next player must then pass the article straight back to the first player and ask, "This is a what?" The first player must then reaffirm his suggestion to the second player by passing the spoon back again saying, "This is a rat!". The second player then continues this sequence with the third player by passing the spoon to him and saying, "This is a rat!", and so the sequence continues. Players are disqualified if they fail to complete a sequence.

If you want to make the game harder you can start another sequence going round the table in the opposite direction.

La-De-Da

The game involves a combination of picking up random objects on the table and banging them down on either side of your place in time to a chant which has to be said or sung correctly by each player. The first player picks up an article, let us say a pepper pot. Beginning by tapping the pot on the right hand side of his place, and then on the left, he must chant as follows:

La-De	RIGHT
Da	LEFT
La-De	RIGHT
Da	LEFT
La-De	RIGHT
Da-De	LEFT
Da-De	RIGHT
Da	LEFT

He then passes the pepper pot to the person on his right who has to complete the chant and the sequence, and so the pepper pot is passed round the table.

If you want to make the game more complicated, as soon as the first player has completed his sequence, he can start again with another article and then pass it to the person on his left. Indeed he can continue to pick up as many articles as there are players seated around the table. This will add to the confusion and, add considerably to the noise.

The Spaghetti Game

This is a very simple, silly game. All you need is a piece of dried spaghetti. Everyone sits in a circle – lady-gentleman-lady-gentleman – around the room. The spaghetti is introduced somewhere into the circle and the object is that, as it is passed from mouth to mouth, a piece must be bitten off each time. The losers are the couple who are closest together at the end without being able to take another bite.

If blackmailing is one of your hobbies, you may wish to photograph the last couple in their close embrace. The spaghetti will not show up in the photograph.

Mess Games

Mess Games

I have tapped military unintelligence sources so that we may all now participate in some of the more outrageous activities which are known to take place in the Officers' Mess. Most of these games are of a violent nature.

Black Knight

All that is required is a large room, a broom and an empty waste paper basket. Someone, preferably a newcomer to the game, is selected to become the Black Knight. At one end of the room, and with the open end facing the Black Knight, the waste paper basket is placed on its side. At the other end, holding the broom handle to his chin, the Black Knight is told to look upwards, along the line of the handle, at the ceiling. He is turned around several times to make him a little giddy and must then charge the wastepaper basket with all the zest and fervour of a mounted, mediaeval knight. The chances of a tanked-up young subaltern scoring a bull's-eye are extremely remote.

It has been known for people to finish up in hospital after a spirited game of Black Knight. See if you can do any better at this indoor jousting contest.

Mess Rugger

In this game a young subaltern assumes the role of a rugger ball. The mess is then divided into two teams and, with rules that will reveal themselves as the game progresses, they each endeavour to carry the subaltern to the opposing wall. As soon as he touches the wall it counts as a try.

Tunnel Rugger

This time a real rugger ball is used. Two teams are selected, with no limit to the numbers. A member of team A begins the line and a member of team B becomes the next in line, turning his back on the member of team A. The next member of team A faces the member of team B and a member of team A faces him and so on to the end of a line (see diagram).

All members of both teams bend over so that they will be able to see the ball shooting up and down between everyone's legs. A referee introduces the ball into the centre of the line and team A must try and pass the ball to one another, endeavouring to throw the ball through all the legs so that it leaves the line in one direction, while team B are trying to achieve the same in the other direction.

A Loon With A Spoon

The object of this game is for two people to blindfold themselves, hold the handle end of a teaspoon in their mouths and take it in turns to bop each other over the head with the spoon. The secret of the game is kept from one of the competitors who, it must be established, does not know the game. So the person who does not know the game is given first strike and, holding the spoon in his mouth, tries to hit his opponent on the top of the head. A referee will announce a hit or a miss. Then it's the turn of the person who does know the game. Instead of making the strike himself, an unblindfolded accomplice holding a serving spoon, bops the first player right on the top of the crown. This sequence continues until the player who does not know the game realises that there's something wrong with the odds as well as with the mysterious power behind his opponent's spoon. See how long it takes for the victim to work it out.

Caterpillars

Two teams are formed, ideally with six people in each, although it is quite possible to have more players if they are available. Team A forms a single-line scrum facing, and about six feet from, a wall, so that there is a line six men long, bent over with each man holding the jacket of the man in front. Team B places one man against the wall facing the Team A scrum or 'caterpillar'. It is Team B's objective to leapfrog and clamber, one by one, over the length of the caterpillar. It is Team A's objective to buck them off. Team A may use any method of bending, contorting and bucking, but no member of the team is allowed to use his hands. When the first member of Team B has ridden the length of the caterpillar, the second member of Team B starts.

The winning team is the one which completes the exercise in the shortest time.

Cock Fighting

This complicated form of fighting takes place with just two players at a time. The two contestants sit facing each other on the floor. Both of them draw their ankles up to their chins and keep their feet together by clasping their arms around the front of their legs. The position is maintained more effectively by fastening the players' ankles together. Both players are given a walking stick, or something similar, which is passed through the legs, under the knees and above the arms. The two combatants must then attempt to throw each other off balance. This is best accomplished by one player getting his feet between the feet of his opponent and giving a swift, upward jerk.

Straw Bales

The mess is divided up into two teams, or two straw bales, as they will become. The teams are bound by a rope tied round all their waists. A course is agreed: over the sofa, under the dining-room table and so on. On the word 'go' the two teams race round the course. In the unlikely event of a team completing the course, they are declared the winners.

Mess Polo

A number of bicycles are commandeered for the occasion, also a number of polo mallets. Divide the players into two teams and play polo within the confines of the mess.

The Tunnel Game

This is an extremely rough game. A tunnel is created by pushing two sofas against each other, back to back. Two teams are formed with four people in each and, starting from opposite ends of the tunnel, they race to get through the tunnel and out the other side. There will be much confrontation in the tunnel which, of course, is the whole point of the game. The most effective way of ensuring that the tunnel remains intact is for a group to lean on either side of the sofas, and push inwards.

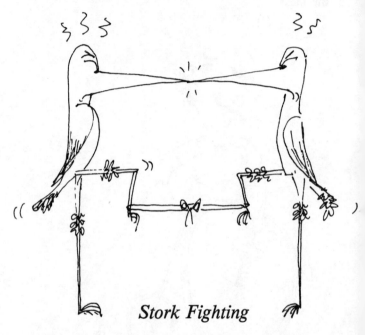

Stork Fighting

The Storks are two players who hop about on their right feet with their left ankles joined by a piece of cord two or three feet long. It is the object of each player to force his opponent to touch the floor with his left foot, and points are scored every time this happens. One way of achieving this is to hop sharply on to your opponent's right foot, which will have the effect of dragging his left foot against his other knee. If a player saves himself with his hand, a point is scored against him all the same.

The Claret Is Mine

Three players get on the inside of a circle of rope or cord approximately six metres long. They each lean back on the rope and hold on to it, thus pulling it taut. A glass of claret is placed in the middle of the circle (or triangle) and each player pulls and heaves with one hand and his body, and tries to pick up the glass of claret. When one player reaches it, he must say, "The claret is mine", and try to drink it. Should he spill any, the glass is recharged and the game begins again. The winner is the last one still standing in the circle.

Over The Top

One team starts on one side of a building and another team starts on the othe side. At the sound of a whistle, or the firing of a flare, the two teams race each other over the building. This game is clearly dangerous. To make it

even more dangerous, you may chose to allow the teams to resist each other's efforts on the roof of the building. On the other hand, you may chose not to do this.

Lancaster Bomber

It is explained that a squadron of Lancasters are returning to base after a night-bombing raid in which much damage was inflicted on the aircraft by anti-aircraft fire. It's going to be a bumpy landing for everyone. Divide the company into two teams (two squadrons). Team A position themselves around a table with a mattress on it and Team B line up in readiness to land on the table. On the word 'go', the first member of Team B must run at the table, leap into the air and attempt a landing on the table. At the same time Team A are rocking it from side to side to make the landing as difficult as possible and to dislodge each player from the table when they have landed.

The winning team is the one which, cumulatively spends the greatest time on the 'runway' before being tossed to the ground.

The Russian Bicycle Ride

WARNING: UNDER NO CIRCUMSTANCES SHOULD YOU EVER PLAY THIS GAME

I am told that this game used to be played in the Officers' Messes of the Imperial Russian Army. It is included here simply as an historical curiosity.

As the title suggests, there is an element of danger involved. The props needed are a shotgun with two cartridges and a bicycle. At the game's outset the shotgun is dismantled and placed on a table and, beside the pieces, are placed the two cartridges. Two subalterns then run a race – six times round a table, six times round the mess, or whatever seems appropriate. The first subaltern to complete the course must mount the bicycle and pedal like hell, out of the mess and as far as he can up the nearest road. The second subaltern, on completing the course, assembles the shotgun, pops the two cartridges into the breach and endeavours to shoot the first subaltern off his bicycle. The way to succeed at this game is to try and be second in the race, thus guaranteeing yourself the superior ironmongery!

Most Wicked Deeds

Most Wicked Deeds

To be properly appreciated, the following wicked ideas should be well planned and carefully executed. A joke which turns sour, either because of bad timing or because of a serious misjudgement of a hostess's sense of humour, can have unpleasant repercussions.

The unfortunate David Hoylake-Johnson in William Douglas-Home's *The Reluctant Debutante* was erroneously credited with the seduction of Brenda Barrington by tempting her with brandy and nuts. Mothers on the circuit wallowed in the scandal until the innocence of the circumstances in which Hoylake-Johnson was discovered in possession of these weapons of seduction were revealed. Here is a modest selection of japes which have been known to take place. Names have been excluded to protect the guilty.

McNab

After the publication of John Buchan's famous book in which the hero, John McNab, bets the owner of a large Scottish estate that he will take, undetected, a salmon, a grouse and a stag off his land in one day, the idea became very fashionable. More recently, with rigid gamekeeping and stringent policing of the rivers, it has become much more difficult. However, it can be done. As recently as last year a young Captain in the Argyll and Sutherland Highlanders got his McNab on the Royal Estate at Balmoral, and has a signed certificate to prove it. His McNab was a little out of the ordinary as he was guarding the place at the time, and he issued no challenge to the residents. But the story goes that he was egged on by a senior member of the Royal Family, and the whole affair caused some consternation – with the Head Keeper in particular.

The rules are simple. Send a letter to the owner of the estate you propose to trespass upon. Tell him the day on which you have decided to perform the feat, and sign the letter 'McNab'. You can be sure that the challenge will be clearly understood and that your rival will be familiar with the book.

If you are detected – and you probably will be – you are throwing yourself at the mercy of the Laird. You also lose the challenge. Should you succeed, you must deliver the game to your rival at the end of the day without being seen. This was once achieved by the 'McNab' posing as a milkman and carrying the game to the front door on the back of a milk float. If the whole venture is successful, and your challenge is accepted by the Laird, he is obliged to give you a signed certificate as proof of your success.

Kidnapping

Surprisingly, this is a very old weekend activity. The idea being to kidnap a member of another house party, offering to return him only if the host can offer tea or pimms, depending on the time of year. The trick is to kidnap someone essential to the continuing success of the house party in question.

Merlin The Marvel

It is a brave man who can carry out this jape successfully and uninjured. As a small boy, an uncle of the illustrator was dispatched instantly to his bed for performing it on a dignified guest.

The trickster bets someone £5 that he can cut his tie into several pieces and then put it back together. Much to the amusement of everyone present, possibly the victim included, 'Merlin' slices the victim's tie into tiny pieces and gives him the remains, together with a £5 note. "You see", explains Merlin, "you win because I can't put your tie back together."

That is the end of the trick. The catch is that it has to be worth a fiver, or whatever the going rate for a good tie.

Kippers

The odour of a kipper lingers even beyond their removal. Consider carefully the victim's plight before making this brutal attack upon his senses.

Under the bonnet of a car, somewhere in the vicinity

of extreme heat, attach the corpse of a kipper. What is so delightfully devious is that the essences takes time to mature. On a journey from Truro to London, a victim may be in Taunton before the aroma seeps through his ventilation system and becomes properly evident. Should you happen to be a guest who is eager to leave a lasting momento of yourself, or be thoroughly dis-enamoured of your host's hospitality, a carefully secured kipper underneath a table near to a radiator will leave a lingering remembrance of your visit for a very long time.

The Long Weight

This is a minor jape which is appropriate to someone who continually fails to lift a finger to help. You will need a worthy accomplice to carry it off successfully. You ask your unhelpful guest, as he lounges in your best armchair, to assist you in 'weighing some things' in such a way as to make it impossible for him to decline. You then take him into the kitchen if you happen to have an aged weighing machine there or you take him into an outhouse where there may be an old machine for weighing potatoes – as long as the machine is an old one which requires real weights to be placed at one end. As you sift through the weights, you remark that one of them is missing. Perhaps, you say to your guest, he would be kind enough to trot down to Arthur's house (your accomplice), who borrowed it off you some weeks ago.

Arthur will be delighted to see a victim arrive and, when he knocks at the door and asks for the weight, Arthur will ask him to wait a minute. Arthur then disappears into his house, never to return. The victim is left to hang on until he realizes that he's been had!

The Rampant Butler

This is best played when you are giving a house party and are expecting some guests for dinner. If one of your party is a proficient actor, this will considerably add to the amusement. He should dress up as your butler but he must be unknown to any of your dinner guests. Finally, you should give your butler a name. Horace is quite a good choice. The idea is that 'Horace's' behaviour throughout the course of the evening should slowly deteriorate. He should also take a lurid fancy to one of the ladies which should become increasingly evident as the evening progresses.

'Horace' can begin his degrading behaviour by announcing dinner with a cigarette hanging from the side of his mouth. During dinner he can help himself to the odd glass of wine and begin his special relationship with the chosen lady. As he offers her some potatoes, some lewd comment about his long-time fascination for big women should raise an eyebrow or two. Over the vegetables, something about how useful it is to be able to see in the dark in a suggestive tone of voice will definitely sow the seeds of concern in the mind of the victim. Should, at any stage, the victim lodge a complaint with her hostess, an embarrassed apology followed by a put-down line like "So difficult to get staff nowadays; Horace was all I could find," will keep her at bay for a while longer. 'Horace' may continue his appalling behaviour by pouring himself a large glass of port, blowing his nose with all his might and lighting a cigar from one of the candles. His grand finale could be to run his fingers through the chosen victim's hair. This is probably the point at which all will have to be revealed to avoid a catastrophe.

A Loo With A View

A devilish jape – place clingfilm over the loo.

A Gnome In The Home

Many people would die if they threw back their curtains one morning to find a bright red gnome, fishing contentedly for nothing in particular, in their garden. If you acquire a gaggle of gnomes and spread them generously around the garden of a proud man, the results will be hilarious. The full effect of this jape will never be known unless you have a 'plant' in the house concerned to pass on the complete results.